HOPE

YOUR HEART'S DEEPEST LONGINGS

JACK
KUHATSCHEK

8 STUDIES
FOR INDIVIDUALS
OR GROUPS

Life
Builder
Study

INTER-VARSITY PRESS
36 Causton Street, London SW1P 4ST, England
Email: ivp@ivpbooks.com
Website: www.ivpbooks.com

Originally published in the United States of America in the LifeGuide® Bible Studies series in 2003 by InterVarsity Press, Downers Grove, Illinois
First published in Great Britain by Scripture Union in 2010
Second edition published in 2015
This edition published in Great Britain by Inter-Varsity Press 2020

British Library Cataloguing-in-Publication Data
A catalogue record for this book is available from the British Library.

ISBN: 978-1-78359-844-1

Printed in Great Britain by Ashford Colour Press Ltd, Gosport, Hampshire

Inter-Varsity Press publishes Christian books that are true to the Bible and that communicate the gospel, develop discipleship and strengthen the church for its mission in the world.

IVP originated within the Inter-Varsity Fellowship, now the Universities and Colleges Christian Fellowship, a student movement connecting Christian Unions in universities and colleges throughout Great Britain, and a member movement of the International Fellowship of Evangelical Students. Website: www.uccf.org.uk. That historic association is maintained, and all senior IVP staff and committee members subscribe to the UCCF Basis of Faith.

Contents

Getting the Most Out of *Hope*

While vacationing in Florida this past spring, our family saw an unusual exhibit at Marineland. It was a tiny, makeshift boat that had washed ashore with no one aboard. The boat, if you could call it a boat, was made from old oil drums that had been lashed together with ropes. A crude steel frame had been constructed over the barrels, while thin sheets of scrap metal and a few planks of old wood had been hammered together for a deck. Toward the front of this pitiful vessel was a wooden mast where once pieces of old cloth had been hand-sewn into a sail. The mast was now as empty as the boat itself. A plaque attached to the side of the boat informed us that it had been constructed by Cuban refugees who had tried to reach the United States but had died during the voyage.

What caused these families to leave their homeland and crowd aboard this feeble raft? Why did they risk their lives making a journey that had so little chance of success? I think the answer can be summed up in one word: hope. They obviously hoped that the United States would offer them far more than the hardship they had known in Cuba. Perhaps they also hoped to be reunited with family members who had somehow made it here safely. Although their voyage ended in tragedy, I'm sure that it began with hopeful expectation.

In some ways their experience can become a parable about our Christian hope, but the parable looks very different depending on your perspective. If we adopt the divine perspective, then we can describe our voyage in a triumphal way. We too have left our old life behind and have set sail for a new and better world. Yet we aren't aboard a makeshift boat but a large and powerful ship that crashes through every wave, weathers the worst of storms and brings us to our desired haven with complete certainty and safety.

To the secular world around us, however, our vessel more closely resembles the one used by the refugees. Our craft is constructed of two wooden beams once lashed together and used to execute a condemned man. Our sail is made from ancient hand-written scrolls and pieces of parchment that describe events that happened two thousand years ago. And our hopes of reaching the land we long for seem foolish and absurd.

If we're honest, we must admit that we sometimes waver between these two perspectives. At times God seems very close, and hope becomes so real that it's almost tangible. But at other times, especially when tragedy or hardship crashes upon us, we wonder whether our hopes will break apart and leave us exposed, vulnerable and overwhelmed.

In this LifeBuilder we will explore both perspectives. We will bring our doubts and fears to the surface and face them honestly. But we will also allow the great hope we have in Jesus Christ to confront our doubts, calm our fears and fill us with joyous anticipation. Welcome aboard!

Suggestions for Individual Study

1. As you begin each study, pray that God will speak to you through his Word.

2. Read the introduction to the study and respond to the personal reflection question or exercise. This is designed to help you focus on God and on the theme of the study.

3. Each study deals with a particular passage—so that you can delve into the author's meaning in that context. Read and reread the passage to be studied. The questions are written using the language of the New International Version, so you may wish to use that version of the Bible. The New Revised Standard Version is also recommended.

4. This is an inductive Bible study, designed to help you discover for yourself what Scripture is saying. The study includes three types of questions. *Observation* questions ask about the basic facts: who, what, when, where and how. *Interpretation* questions delve into the meaning of the passage. *Application* questions help you discover the implications of the text for growing in Christ. These three keys unlock the treasures of Scripture.

Write your answers to the questions in the spaces provided or in a personal journal. Writing can bring clarity and deeper understanding of yourself and of God's Word.

5. It might be good to have a Bible dictionary handy. Use it to look up any unfamiliar words, names or places.

6. Use the prayer suggestion to guide you in thanking God for what you have learned and to pray about the applications that have come to mind.

7. You may want to go on to the suggestion under "Now or Later," or you may want to use that idea for your next study.

Suggestions for Members of a Group Study

1. Come to the study prepared. Follow the suggestions for individual study mentioned above. You will find that careful preparation will greatly enrich your time spent in group discussion.

2. Be willing to participate in the discussion. The leader of your group will not be lecturing. Instead, he or she will be encouraging the members of the group to discuss what they have learned. The leader will be asking the questions that are found in this guide.

3. Stick to the topic being discussed. Your answers should be based on the verses which are the focus of the discussion and not on outside authorities such as commentaries or speakers. These studies focus on a particular passage of Scripture. Only rarely should you refer to other portions of the Bible. This allows for everyone to participate in in-depth study on equal ground.

4. Be sensitive to the other members of the group. Listen attentively when they describe what they have learned. You may be surprised by their insights! Each question assumes a variety of answers. Many questions do not have "right" answers, particularly questions that aim at meaning or application. Instead the questions push us to explore the passage more thoroughly.

When possible, link what you say to the comments of others. Also, be affirming whenever you can. This will encourage some of the more hesitant members of the group to participate.

5. Be careful not to dominate the discussion. We are sometimes so eager to express our thoughts that we leave too little opportunity for others to respond. By all means participate! But allow others to also.

6. Expect God to teach you through the passage being discussed and through the other members of the group. Pray that you will have an enjoyable and profitable time together, but also that as a result of the study you will find ways that you can take action individually and/or as a group.

7. Remember that anything said in the group is considered confidential and should not be discussed outside the group unless specific permission is given to do so.

8. If you are the group leader, you will find additional suggestions at the back of the guide.

1

Waiting
for the Lord

One of Samuel Beckett's most famous plays is entitled *Waiting for Godot*. Throughout the play the characters wait and wait for Godot to appear, but he never does. The play is Beckett's way of saying that hope is futile—especially hope in God.

GROUP DISCUSSION. In what kinds of situations do you find it hardest to wait?

PERSONAL REFLECTION. Think of a time when you waited on the Lord to answer a prayer. What did you learn through that experience?

In contrast to Beckett's despair, the Bible offers hope to those who are fearful or oppressed. When we feel overwhelmed and

ready to give up, Psalm 27 encourages us to "wait for the
LORD." When we see no possibility of relief, David assures us,
"I am still confident of this: I will see the goodness of the LORD
in the land of the living." *Read Psalm 27.*

---

1. David's confidence in this prayer is based on God's promises
to him in 2 Samuel 7:5-16 (see also v. 28). What specific items
in the psalm are related to God's promises to David?

---

2. Why must our hope be based on God's promises?

What have you seen happen in your life or in the lives of others
when we do not base our hope in God?

---

3. David is able to be fearless in the face of evil men, armies
and even war (vv. 1-3). Describe his attitude.

---

4. What images of safety does David apply to the Lord in verses
1-2 and 5-6?

How do these images give you hope?

---

5. David seeks not only the Lord's protection but also the Lord himself (v. 4). How is David's intense desire for God revealed in this psalm?

---

6. What would it mean for us to "dwell in the house of the LORD" (v. 4), "gaze upon the beauty of the LORD" (v. 4), and "seek his face" (v. 8)?

---

7. David's confident statements about the Lord (vv. 1-6) lead up to his prayer in verses 7-12. What is the substance of that prayer?

What real dangers does he seem to be facing?

8. The psalm ends as it begins—with David's confidence in the Lord's help (vv. 13-14). How can David's view of God help you to "be strong and take heart" when you are fearful or facing difficult circumstances?

---

9. Why must your hope not only be confident but also patient (v. 14)?

How have your experiences of waiting for the Lord strengthened you?

Ask God to strengthen your confidence in his goodness and to make you patient as you wait for his help.

Now or Later

Read Psalm 27 in one of the newer translations, such as The Message or the New Living Translation. What new insights do you gain from reading this psalm in a different translation?

2

Renewing
Your Strength

Isaiah 40:25-31

In the movie *Chariots of Fire*, there is a scene in which Scottish athlete Eric Liddell is racing against some of his countrymen. During the early part of the race, another runner bumps him, and Liddell falls forward with his arms outstretched and crashes against the turf. Onlookers groan disappointedly, assuming that he is out of the race. But even though the other runners are twenty yards ahead, Liddell gets up and begins sprinting at top speed toward the pack. As they come to the final stretch, he passes one runner after another and then, in typical fashion, throws his head back and sprints victorious across the finish line. Although Liddell collapses exhausted in the arms of his friends, everyone knows from that day on that he is destined for greatness.

GROUP DISCUSSION. Have you ever felt like giving up on a task because you were too tired, weak or discouraged? Explain.

PERSONAL REFLECTION. How were you able to complete a task recently that seemed more than you could handle?

In everyone's life there are times when we stumble and fall, when we are so weary and discouraged that we feel we cannot go on. During such times, where can we find the strength to get back up and complete the race? In Isaiah 40 the prophet tells us not to give up but to put our hope in the Lord. *Read Isaiah 40:25-31.*

---

1. During their captivity in Babylon, why might the Israelites compare their God to the gods of their captors (v. 25)?

---

2. When we are defeated or discouraged, why do we tend to question God's power?

---

3. In verse 26 God urges his people to lift up their eyes and look at the starry hosts. How can meditating on God's creation, especially the vastness and beauty of the universe, renew our confidence in his power?

---

4. Why would being held captive for seventy years in a foreign land cause the Israelites to complain and to question God's concern for them (v. 27)?

5. When something bad happens to you, are you more likely to question God's power or his love and concern for you? Explain.

6. During the times when we question God's care, why do we need a fresh vision of his power, strength and wisdom (v. 28)?

7. In what ways do you struggle with feeling tired, weak, weary or faint (vv. 29-31)?

How might your weakened condition cause you to stumble and fall (v. 30)?

8. What does it mean to "hope in the LORD" (v. 31)—especially when we think we cannot go on?

9. How do the images of a soaring eagle, a runner and even a walker help us understand God's promise to renew our strength (v. 31)?

10. How does Isaiah's portrait of God encourage you and give you hope?

---

11. At this point in your life what help do you need from God in order to run and not grow weary?

Thank God for the strength he gives you to walk, run and even soar like an eagle when you put your hope and trust in him.

Now or Later

In Isaiah 40:26 the Lord tells us:

> Lift your eyes and look to the heavens:
>> Who created all these?
> He who brings out the starry host one by one,
>> and calls them each by name.
> Because of his great power and mighty strength,
>> not one of them is missing.

Spend time this week meditating on some aspect of God's creation, such as the stars and planets. Write about how this experience gives you a greater appreciation of his great power and strength.

3

Investing
in the Future

1 Timothy 6:3-19

One of the darkest periods in modern financial history began on October 24, 1929. During a six-day period the value of securities dropped by 26 billion dollars. By the end of November the nationwide loss exceeded 100 billion dollars. According to the Grolier Encyclopedia, by 1933 "over fourteen million Americans were unemployed, industrial production was down to one-third of its 1929 level, and national income had dropped by more than half."

GROUP DISCUSSION. Imagine that your country experienced a Great Depression. How do you think your life would be different? (Or think about winning the lottery or a sweepstakes. How would your life change if you won?)

PERSONAL REFLECTION. In what areas are you tempted to put your trust in circumstances more than in God?

In 1 Timothy 6:3-19 Paul warns us against putting our hope in wealth, "which is so uncertain." Instead, he urges us to invest our time, resources and energy in the only future which is eternally secure. *Read 1 Timothy 6:3-19.*

---

1. What are the qualities of a godly person according to this passage?

Godly Person Contentment great gain

---

2. One of the marks of a false teacher is that he thinks "godliness is a means to financial gain" (vv. 3-5). Why might greed lead to false teaching?

---

3. According to Paul, the godly person should be content with merely food and clothing (vv. 6-8). How does this view contrast with society's requirements for contentment?

How do you relate to each of these views (Paul's and the world's)?

4. What dangers and difficulties await those who love money and want to get rich (vv. 9-10)?

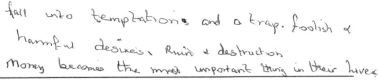

fall into temptations and a trap. foolish &
harmful desires, Ruin & destruction
Money becomes the most important thing in their lives

5. How might the desire for riches lead people into temptation, ruin, destruction and grief—and even cause them to wander from the faith?

6. Even though people around us may devote their lives to accumulating wealth, what higher calling does Paul urge us to pursue (vv. 11-16)?

7. How can wealth lead to arrogance and a false sense of security (v. 17)?

8. Paul's warnings against wealth might lead us to think God is a miserly killjoy. Yet how does Paul's description of God in verse 17 shatter that notion?

Why is it so important to put our hope in the Provider rather than in what he richly provides?

---

9. According to Paul, what is the best investment strategy for a secure future (vv. 18-19)?

---

10. What adjustments do you need to make in your lifestyle or giving patterns to better follow Paul's investment strategy?

Thank God for richly providing everything for our enjoyment. Ask him to set you free from the love of money so that you can pursue true riches and discover "the life that is truly life" (v. 19).

Now or Later
One of the best ways to free yourself from the grip of possessions is to give them away. This week write a check to one of your favorite charities, or give some of your clothes to Goodwill.

4

Living in Hope

When I was a kid, my parents decided to take our family to Disneyland. As the day drew closer, my sense of excitement and anticipation mounted. I had never seen Disneyland in person, but I had heard about it for years. I had listened to Walt Disney himself describe the wonders of Tomorrowland, Adventureland and Main Street USA. I had seen films of the Mouseketeers sailing on a sternwheeler, peering out a porthole in Captain Nemo's submarine and screaming as they rode the runaway mine train. To me it sounded like the best place on earth! The anticipation was nearly as much fun as the trip itself.

GROUP DISCUSSION. When you know that something wonderful is about to happen—an exciting vacation, the birth of a child, a visit from your best friend—how does your sense of anticipation affect you?

PERSONAL REFLECTION. How do wonderful experiences here on earth increase your appreciation for God's goodness?

In 1 Peter 1 the apostle describes both a person and a place we've never seen—a place so exciting and a person so wonderful that we should be filled with a childlike sense of joy and anticipation. *Read 1 Peter 1:3-12.*

1. According to Peter, what are some of the reasons we have for praising God (vv. 3-5)?

2. How has Christ's resurrection from the dead given us a "living hope" (v. 3)?

3. How would your life and attitudes change if you were told you had inherited a vast fortune from a long-lost relative?

How can the excitement and joy of an earthly inheritance help us to look forward to the greater inheritance God has promised us in heaven (v. 4)?

4. How do trials of various kinds prove the reality of our faith in Jesus Christ (vv. 6-7)?

5. What kinds of trials have demonstrated that your faith is genuine?

6. Do you find it difficult to believe in and love a Savior you've never seen (vv. 8-9)? Explain.

7. When Peter speaks of the salvation of our souls (v. 9), he is thinking of our whole person—body, mind, spirit and everything else that makes us human. What excites you most about the hope of experiencing a *total* personal renewal?

8. How were the Old Testament prophets serving future generations when they spoke of the sufferings of Christ and the glories that would follow (vv. 10-12)?

9. Peter concludes this passage with a brief and somewhat odd remark: "Even angels long to look into these things" (v. 12). Why do you think he felt this was worth mentioning?

How might that help you hold on to hope today?

Take a moment to reflect on the magnitude of what Peter has described in this passage. Spend time thanking and praising God for the incredible hope we have in Jesus Christ.

Now or Later

Get out a photo album that shows pictures of one of your favorite vacations or places to visit. How do such times here on earth increase your desire for the joys of heaven?

5

Longing for Glory

The Bible tells us that receiving glory is one of our greatest hopes. But for many of us this hope is vague and confusing because we don't have a clue as to what heavenly glory is. Even the brilliant C. S. Lewis wrote (in *The Weight of Glory*): "Glory suggests two ideas to me, of which one seems wicked and the other ridiculous. Either glory means to me fame, or it means luminosity. As for the first, since to be famous means to be better known than other people, the desire for fame appears to me as a competitive passion and therefore of hell rather than heaven. As for the second, who wishes to become a kind of living electric light bulb?"

GROUP DISCUSSION. What images or ideas come to mind when you think of the word *glory*?

PERSONAL REFLECTION. In what ways are you encouraged by the hope of glory in heaven?

In Romans 8 Paul helps us to figure out what heavenly glory is, so that we can become more excited and expectant about it. He also encourages us to look beyond our present sufferings and groanings to the glorious hope that awaits us in Jesus Christ. *Read Romans 8:18-27.*

---

1. As you look over this passage, what key words express the difficulties of this present time?

---

2. In verse 18 Paul isn't speaking about suffering in general but rather about the sufferings we experience for Jesus' sake (see v. 17). In what ways have you suffered because of your faith in Jesus Christ?

---

3. Verses 20-22 say that the whole of creation is subject to frustration, bondage to decay and groaning. What evidence do you see of this in the world today?

---

4. What do you think Paul means when he declares that all of creation will be "liberated from its bondage to decay" and "brought into the glorious freedom of the children of God" (v. 21)?

5. Sometimes the Christian life is presented as nothing but joy and spiritual bliss. Yet in what sense is an inner groaning—as in the pains of childbirth—part of normal Christian experience (v. 23)?

6. Paul uses four expressions to describe what we long for and eagerly await: "the glory that will be revealed in us" (v. 18); "the glorious freedom of the children of God" (v. 21); "our adoption as sons" (v. 23); "the redemption of our bodies" (v. 23). How do these expressions help you understand our future hope?

7. Biblical hope isn't wishful thinking, as in "I hope I win the lottery." How does Paul define *hope* in verses 24-25?

Why should this kind of hope be a key component of our Christian lives?

8. Even in the midst of great hope we still have weaknesses and human limitations (v. 26). How does the Holy Spirit help us with these (vv. 26-27)?

How does this ministry of the Holy Spirit encourage you and give you hope?

9. How would you summarize the ways our present life on earth contrasts with our future life?

10. Describe one or two ways our glorious hope could transform your present attitude or lifestyle.

Thank God for the glorious hope that awaits us as his children. Pray that an eager and vibrant hope will characterize your life here on earth.

Now or Later

In 2 Corinthians 4:16-18 Paul writes: "Therefore we do not lose heart. Though outwardly we are wasting away, yet inwardly we are being renewed day by day. For our light and momentary troubles are achieving for us an eternal glory that far outweighs them all. So we fix our eyes not on what is seen, but on what is unseen. For what is seen is temporary, but what is unseen is eternal." Underline all of the contrasts (such as *outwardly* versus *inwardly*) that you see in this passage. How do these contrasts help you appreciate the hope we have in Christ?

6

The Ultimate Victory

On November 22, 1963, we arrived at Love Field just as Air Force One was landing. We made our way through the crowd and pressed our faces against a chainlink fence, waiting for the door of the plane to open. I still have a vivid memory of the scene we've all watched on television so many times since then. President Kennedy emerged with his thick hair and big smile. Jackie had on a pink suit and her trademark pillbox hat. They waved to the crowd and then came over and shook hands with many of the people. We all felt like we were seeing royalty! Then they got into the black limousine and drove away.

After we stopped for lunch on the way home, an announcer came on the radio and said that Kennedy had been shot. Then a few minutes later he said, "The President of the United States is dead." We were all in shock. We had just seen Kennedy thirty minutes before, and now he was dead!

That was the first time in my life that I understood the reality of human mortality.

GROUP DISCUSSION. When have you come face-to-face with your own mortality or that of someone you loved?

PERSONAL REFLECTION. How does your own mortality affect your outlook on life?

It is right and natural to grieve when we lose someone we love. Even Jesus wept at the tomb of Lazarus. But Paul tells us not to grieve as others do who have no hope, because in Jesus Christ we have the great and encouraging hope of the resurrection. In 1 Corinthians 15, we'll explore that hope in some detail. *Read 1 Corinthians 15:35-58.*

1. In verse 35 someone asks, "How are the dead raised? With what kind of body will they come?" How would you summarize Paul's answer (vv. 36-41)?

2. According to Paul, how will our future bodies be radically different from our present ones (vv. 42-44)?

3. It's fun to fantasize about our resurrection bodies. If you could have the body you've always wanted, what would it be like?

4. How do the differences between Adam and Christ further illustrate the differences between our present bodies and our future ones (vv. 44-49)?

5. Suppose that in the next ten years they invent an anti-aging pill that would allow you to live to be 700, 800 or even 900 years old like some of the early biblical characters. Would you take the pill? Why or why not?

6. Even if a pill could enable us to live indefinitely, in what ways are our present bodies unfit for the kingdom of God (vv. 50, 53)?

7. How would you explain the details of the mystery Paul describes in verses 51-52?

8. In verse 55, Paul paraphrases Hosea 13:14: "Where, O death, is your victory? Where, O death, is your sting?" How has Christ both conquered death and removed its sting (vv. 54-56)?

9. How does Christ's victory over death strengthen your faith and fill your heart with thanks to God (vv. 57-58)?

10. How does the resurrection also make all the difference between meaningful work here on earth and meaningless, futile work (v. 58)?

11. Many people have an intense fear of death. How does Paul's teaching about the resurrection ease your fears and give you hope?

Thank God for the hope of the resurrection. Pray that your life will be transformed by that hope.

Now or Later
Read Paul's defense before Agrippa in Acts 25:23—26:32. What do you learn about Paul's belief in the resurrection and the affect it had on his life?

7

The Return of
the King

Several years ago a major Christian publishing house decided
to issue a revised edition of a book on prophecy. Soon after the
book was released, the Gulf War began. It was a publisher's
dream come true! People began to wonder whether the Gulf
War was somehow related to biblical prophecy about the end of
the world and the second coming of Jesus Christ.

Sales of the book went through the roof: ten thousand, then
fifty thousand, then one hundred thousand, then five hundred
thousand. At its peak, the book sold over a million copies! But
when the Gulf War ended and the world didn't, guess what—
sales of the book stopped immediately. In fact, the publisher
received over 200,000 returned copies.

Why is it that we only seem interested in the Lord's coming
if someone sets a date, or claims that current events are fulfilling biblical prophecy, or if we think Armageddon is just
around the corner? But if things return to normal, then we
put our hope in the second coming back on the shelf—like

that book on prophecy—and forget about it! Jesus never intended for it to be this way.

GROUP DISCUSSION. Why does it often take a world crisis to get Christians thinking about the second coming?

PERSONAL REFLECTION. What influence do world events have on your thoughts about Christ's return?

As we'll see in 1 Thessalonians, the Lord wants the second coming to be a living hope for us that *restructures* our thinking and *reorders* our lives. *Read 1 Thessalonians 4:13—5:11.*

---

1. Three times in this passage, Paul speaks of those who have fallen asleep (4:13, 14, 15). For Christians, why is sleep an appropriate way to describe death?

---

2. When a loved one dies, grief is a natural and appropriate response. But how is our grief to be different those "who have no hope" (4:13-14)?

---

3. According to "the Lord's own word," what sequence of events will occur at his coming (4:15-17)?

How can we encourage each other—especially those who have lost friends or family members—with these words (4:18)?

4. William Miller predicted that the world would end in 1844. Edgar Whisenant, a former NASA engineer, predicted it would end in 1988. Yet according to Paul, why is it foolish to predict the times and dates of the Lord's return (5:1-3)?

5. How should the "sons of the light and sons of the day" be different from the sons of the darkness and sons of the night—both in thinking and in behavior (5:4-8)?

6. How can the command "be alert" (5:6) help us to be ready for Christ's return?

How about "be self-controlled" (5:6, 8)?

"Put on faith and love . . . and the hope of salvation" (5:8)?

---

7. All of humanity will either "suffer wrath" or "receive salvation through our Lord Jesus Christ" (5:9). How could these realities affect the way you relate to your non-Christian friends?

---

8. In what specific ways can we "encourage one another" and "build each other up" (5:11) because of our hope in the Lord's return?

Pray that the Lord will enable you to encourage and strengthen your brothers and sisters in Christ because of the hope of his coming.

Now or Later
Pray for your non-Christian friends this week who have no hope of life after death. Ask God to give you opportunities to talk with them about your hope in Christ.

8

When All Things Become New

In his book *Inside Out*, Dr. Larry Crabb describes one of our deepest inner longings:

> Beneath the surface of everyone's life, especially the more mature, is an ache that will not go away. It can be ignored, disguised, mislabeled, or submerged by a torrent of activity, but it will not disappear. And for good reason. We were designed to enjoy a better world than this. And until that better world comes along, we will *groan* for what we do not have. (*Inside Out* [Colorado Springs: NavPress, 1988], p. 14.)

GROUP DISCUSSION. What one or two things are you looking forward to *most* about heaven, and why?

PERSONAL REFLECTION. In what ways do you experience a taste of heaven here on earth?

In this study we are going to look at that better world—what the Bible calls heaven. We're going to walk around in it, smell the flowers and drink the water, in order to see why heaven holds such an incredible hope for those of us who believe in Jesus Christ. *Read Revelation 21:1-8.*

1. As the scene opens in verses 1-4, what are some of the things John sees and hears?

2. In verse 1, John sees not only a new heaven but also a new earth. What aspects of our present earth would you enjoy seeing again in the renewed, renovated earth?

3. In verse 2 our eternal home is described both as a city and a bride—images that speak of our longings for community and intimacy. What is appealing to you about living forever in close community with others?

How do you think marriage reflects the kind of intimacy we will experience in heaven?

4. According to verse 3, heaven isn't primarily a place but a Person. Why is God the only one who can satisfy our deepest longings?

---

5. In what ways will the old order of things pass away in heaven (vv. 4-5)?

---

6. If God were to wipe away your tears right now—the things that bring you pain or grief or sadness—what would some of those things be?

---

7. The Bible often compares our inner longings to thirst (v. 6; see also John 4:13-14; 7:37-39). How do people try to satisfy that thirst in the wrong ways?

How does it help you to know that your thirst can only be fully quenched in heaven?

8. How do John's words in verse 8 stand in stark contrast to the beauty and perfection described in verses 1-7?

---

9. How do you respond to the idea that not everyone will participate in the glories of heaven?

---

10. John repeatedly describes Christians as those who "overcome" (v. 7; see also Revelation 2:7, 11, 17, 26; 3:5, 12, 21). What challenges do you need to overcome as you await your glorious inheritance?

Take time now to thank God for the day when all things will become new. Ask him for grace to live your life here on earth in light of heavenly realities.

Now or Later
Reread some of the passages covered in this study guide. Which ones had the greatest affect on your hope in Christ, and why?

Leader's Notes

Leading a Bible discussion can be an enjoyable and rewarding experience. But it can also be *scary*—especially if you've never done it before. If this is your feeling, you're in good company. When God asked Moses to lead the Israelites out of Egypt, he replied, "O Lord, please send someone else to do it"! (Ex 4:13). It was the same with Solomon, Jeremiah and Timothy, but God helped these people in spite of their weaknesses, and he will help you as well.

You don't need to be an expert on the Bible or a trained teacher to lead a Bible discussion. The idea behind these inductive studies is that the leader guides group members to discover for themselves what the Bible has to say. This method of learning will allow group members to remember much more of what is said than a lecture would.

These studies are designed to be led easily. As a matter of fact, the flow of questions through the passage from observation to interpretation to application is so natural that you may feel that the studies lead themselves. This study guide is also flexible. You can use it with a variety of groups—student, professional, neighborhood or church groups. Each study takes forty-five to sixty minutes in a group setting.

There are some important facts to know about group dynamics and encouraging discussion. The suggestions listed below should enable you to effectively and enjoyably fulfill your role as leader.

Preparing for the Study

1. Ask God to help you understand and apply the passage in your

own life. Unless this happens, you will not be prepared to lead others. Pray too for the various members of the group. Ask God to open your hearts to the message of his Word and motivate you to action.

2. Read the introduction to the entire guide to get an overview of the entire book and the issues which will be explored.

3. As you begin each study, read and reread the assigned Bible passage to familiarize yourself with it.

4. This study guide is based on the New International Version of the Bible. It will help you and the group if you use this translation as the basis for your study and discussion.

5. Carefully work through each question in the study. Spend time in meditation and reflection as you consider how to respond.

6. Write your thoughts and responses in the space provided in the study guide. This will help you to express your understanding of the passage clearly.

7. It might help to have a Bible dictionary handy. Use it to look up any unfamiliar words, names or places. (For additional help on how to study a passage, see chapter five of *How to Lead a LifeBuilder Study,* IVP, 2018.)

8. Consider how you can apply the Scripture to your life. Remember that the group will follow your lead in responding to the studies. They will not go any deeper than you do.

9. Once you have finished your own study of the passage, familiarize yourself with the leader's notes for the study you are leading. These are designed to help you in several ways. First, they tell you the purpose the study guide author had in mind when writing the study. Take time to think through how the study questions work together to accomplish that purpose. Second, the notes provide you with additional background information or suggestions on group dynamics for various questions. This information can be useful when people have difficulty understanding or answering a question. Third, the leader's notes can alert you to potential problems you may encounter during the study.

10. If you wish to remind yourself of anything mentioned in the leader's notes, make a note to yourself below that question in the study.

Leading the Study

1. Begin the study on time. Open with prayer, asking God to help the group to understand and apply the passage.

2. Be sure that everyone in your group has a study guide. Encourage the group to prepare beforehand for each discussion by reading the introduction to the guide and by working through the questions in the study.

3. At the beginning of your first time together, explain that these studies are meant to be discussions, not lectures. Encourage the members of the group to participate. However, do not put pressure on those who may be hesitant to speak during the first few sessions. You may want to suggest the following guidelines to your group.

☐ Stick to the topic being discussed.

☐ Your responses should be based on the verses which are the focus of the discussion and not on outside authorities such as commentaries or speakers.

☐ These studies focus on a particular passage of Scripture. Only rarely should you refer to other portions of the Bible. This allows for everyone to participate in in-depth study on equal ground.

☐ Anything said in the group is considered confidential and will not be discussed outside the group unless specific permission is given to do so.

☐ We will listen attentively to each other and provide time for each person present to talk.

☐ We will pray for each other.

4. Have a group member read the introduction at the beginning of the discussion.

5. Every session begins with a group discussion question. The question or activity is meant to be used before the passage is read. The question introduces the theme of the study and encourages group members to begin to open up. Encourage as many members as possible to participate, and be ready to get the discussion going with your own response.

This section is designed to reveal where our thoughts or feelings need to be transformed by Scripture. That is why it is especially important not to read the passage before the discussion question is asked. The passage will tend to color the honest reactions people would otherwise give because they are, of course, supposed to think the way the Bible does.

You may want to supplement the group discussion question with an icebreaker to help people to get comfortable. See the community section of the *Small Group Starter Kit* (IVP, 1995) for more ideas.

You also might want to use the personal reflection question with your group. Either allow a time of silence for people to respond individually or discuss it together.

6. Have a group member (or members if the passage is long) read aloud the passage to be studied. Then give people several minutes to read the passage again silently so that they can take it all in.

7. Question 1 will generally be an overview question designed to briefly survey the passage. Encourage the group to look at the whole passage, but try to avoid getting sidetracked by questions or issues that will be addressed later in the study.

8. As you ask the questions, keep in mind that they are designed to be used just as they are written. You may simply read them aloud. Or you may prefer to express them in your own words.

There may be times when it is appropriate to deviate from the study guide. For example, a question may have already been answered. If so, move on to the next question. Or someone may raise an important question not covered in the guide. Take time to discuss it, but try to keep the group from going off on tangents.

9. Avoid answering your own questions. If necessary, repeat or rephrase them until they are clearly understood. Or point out something you read in the leader's notes to clarify the context or meaning. An eager group quickly becomes passive and silent if they think the leader will do most of the talking.

10. Don't be afraid of silence. People may need time to think about the question before formulating their answers.

11. Don't be content with just one answer. Ask, "What do the rest of you think?" or "Anything else?" until several people have given answers to the question.

12. Acknowledge all contributions. Try to be affirming whenever possible. Never reject an answer. If it is clearly off-base, ask, "Which verse led you to that conclusion?" or again, "What do the rest of you think?"

13. Don't expect every answer to be addressed to you, even though this will probably happen at first. As group members become more at ease, they will begin to truly interact with each other. This is one sign of healthy discussion.

14. Don't be afraid of controversy. It can be very stimulating. If you don't resolve an issue completely, don't be frustrated. Move on and keep it in mind for later. A subsequent study may solve the problem.

15. Periodically summarize what the group has said about the passage. This helps to draw together the various ideas mentioned and gives continuity to the study. But don't preach.

16. At the end of the Bible discussion you may want to allow group members a time of quiet to work on an idea under "Now or Later." Then discuss what you experienced. Or you may want to encourage group members to work on these ideas between meetings. Give an opportunity during the session for people to talk about what they are learning.

17. Conclude your time together with conversational prayer, adapting the prayer suggestion at the end of the study to your group. Ask for God's help in following through on the commitments you've made.

18. End on time.

Many more suggestions and helps are found in *How to Lead a LifeBuilder Study.*

Components of Small Groups

A healthy small group should do more than study the Bible. There are four components to consider as you structure your time together.

Nurture. Small groups help us to grow in our knowledge and love of God. Bible study is the key to making this happen and is the foundation of your small group.

Community. Small groups are a great place to develop deep friendships with other Christians. Allow time for informal interaction before and after each study. Plan activities and games that will help you get to know each other. Spend time having fun together—going on a picnic or cooking dinner together.

Worship and prayer. Your study will be enhanced by spending time praising God together in prayer or song. Pray for each other's needs—and keep track of how God is answering prayer in your group. Ask God to help you to apply what you are learning in your study.

Outreach. Reaching out to others can be a practical way of applying what you are learning, and it will keep your group from becoming self-focused. Host a series of evangelistic discussions for your friends or neighbors. Clean up the yard of an elderly friend. Serve at a soup kitchen together, or spend a day working in the community.

Many more suggestions and helps in each of these areas are found in the *Small Group Starter Kit.* You will also find information on building a small group. Reading through the starter kit will be worth your time.

Study 1. Waiting for the Lord. Psalm 27.

Purpose: To encourage us to "wait for the Lord" when we feel over-whelmed or ready to give up.

Group discussion. Every study begins with a discussion question, which is meant to be asked before the passage is read. These questions are important for several reasons.

First, they help the group to warm up to each other. No matter how well a group may know each other, there is always a stiffness that needs to be overcome before people will begin to talk openly. A good question will break the ice.

Second, the questions get people thinking along the lines of the topic of the study. Most people will have lots of different things going on in their minds (dinner, an important meeting coming up, how to get the car fixed) that will have nothing to do with the study. A creative question will get their attention and draw them into the discussion.

Third, the questions can reveal where our thoughts or feelings need to be transformed by Scripture. That is why it is especially important not to read the passage before the questions are asked.

Personal reflection. These questions are designed for individuals studying on their own. If you wish, you could allow group members to silently reflect on the question. Then you could ask a general question about what they experienced in their time of personal reflection (rather than having them answer the question aloud). Or, you could simply move on to the Scripture reading.

Question 1. David's assurance that he has nothing to fear from his enemies (vv. 1-3) is based on God's promise in 2 Samuel 7:11. His confidence that he will see the goodness of the Lord in the land of the living (v. 13) is based on the promises in 2 Samuel 7:9-16. God had promised that David's name would be great, Israel would be established in the land, David would have rest from his enemies, he would have offspring and his kingdom would be established forever. These promises gave David great confidence in times of stress and affliction.

Question 2. Our faith, too, must be grounded in God's promises. Sometimes we are told that if our faith is strong enough or if we "name it and claim it" God will definitely answer our prayers. Yet such assumptions can be naive. John tells us, "This is the confidence we have in approaching God: that if we ask anything according to his will, he hears us. And if we know that he hears us—whatever we ask—we know that we have what we asked of him" (1 Jn 5:14-15). Only those prayers that are according to God's will are answered. And the best way to know God's will is to look at what he commanded and promised in his Word.

Question 4. The word *light* (v. 1) often symbolized well-being and life (see Ps 97:11). A *stronghold* was a fortress that protected people from their enemies. David knew, therefore, that God was the source of his life and well-being, his savior from all potential harm, and his protection from his enemies. David also refers to the Lord as the one who keeps him safe, who hides and shelters him, and who will exalt him (vv. 5-6).

Question 5. David's primary prayer in this psalm is not for protection but rather for the privilege of dwelling in the house of the Lord all the days of his life (v. 4). He desires nothing more than to seek the Lord (vv. 4, 8) and to gaze on his beauty (v. 4). David also wants to learn from the Lord and be guided by him so that he can walk in "a straight path" (v. 11). These are the requests of a man who is passionately devoted to his God.

Question 7. "Hear my voice . . . be merciful to me" (v. 7); "Do not hide your face from me, do not turn your servant away in anger" (v. 9); "Do not reject me or forsake me" (v. 9); "Do not turn me over to the desire of my foes" (v. 12). These are the prayers of a man who seeks deliverance from real and present dangers.

What are those dangers? The psalm mentions enemies in verses 2 and 6. An attacking army and war are mentioned in verse 3. Foes and false witnesses are described in verse 12.

Question 9. Hebrews 11:1 tells us that "faith is being sure of what we hope for and certain of what we do not see." By faith, David was confident that his prayers would be answered, but he also knew that he needed to wait patiently for those answers. Genuine faith does not expect or demand instant results.

Study 2. Renewing Your Strength. Isaiah 40:25-31.

Purpose: To discover how we can renew our strength when we feel weary and discouraged.

Question 1. The "starry host" was also worshiped by the Babylonians, and possibly by some of the Israelites. Isaiah urges the people to look beyond the incredible splendor of the heavens to the God who created the stars and upholds them by his mighty power.

Question 3. If you have ever been in the country on a clear night, you have noticed that the heavens sparkle with stars not visible in the city. With your eyes you can see about 2,000 stars. With 7-power binoculars you can see 50,000 stars. And with a 3-inch telescope you can see hundreds of thousands. The red giant, Betelgeuse, is so far away that the light we see from it first left the star before Columbus sailed for America! If you were able to travel at 186,000 miles per second, it would take you over 100,000 years just to travel across our galaxy, the Milky Way. And yet ours is just one of countless galaxies in the universe. In fact, astronomers believe the universe extends from earth for at least 10 billion light-years. If the greatness of the universe seems incomprehensible, how much more the greatness of the God who created it! (See Roy A. Gallant, *Our Universe* [Washington, D.C.: National Geographic Society, 1980].)

Question 4. Israel had been taken captive in Babylon because of their sin and rebellion, not because God did not care for them. In fact, having stressed God's majesty in verses 12-26, Isaiah devotes the rest of the chapter to God's goodness and care for his people.

Questions 5-6. The fact of evil in the universe—including the evil that affects our lives—has caused some philosophers to pose the following dilemma: "If God is good, then he must not be all powerful; if he is all powerful, then he must not be good." Yet the Bible affirms that God is both all powerful and good. When we blame God for the evil in the world, we forget the fact that it was through humanity's sin and rebellion that evil entered the world (see Gen 3). God is not the author of evil but rather seeks to deliver those who trust in his goodness, wisdom and power.

Questions 7-8. The word *renew* is used for exchanging one set of clothes for another. Those who put their trust in the Lord, who wait patiently and expectantly for his deliverance, will exchange their weakness for strength.

Study 3. Investing in the Future. 1 Timothy 6:3-19.
Purpose: To learn to invest our time, resources and energy in the only future which is eternally secure.

Question 2. In the first century, many philosophers and religious teachers traveled from place to place, charging money for the service they rendered (see 2 Cor 2:17). The popularity of their teaching had a direct affect on their income, so they would make sure their message was acceptable and appealing to their audience. Because these teachers were far more interested in money than truth, their teaching was often heretical.

Paul refused to accept money for his ministry (2 Cor 11:7-15), preferring to support himself and those who worked with him. By doing this Paul achieved four goals: (1) He was not a burden to those to whom he preached (2 Cor 11:9); (2) he did not hinder the gospel, because he avoided the charge that he was only interested in money (2 Cor 2:17); (3) he was an example to others of hard work and generosity (Acts 20:33-35); and (4) he became entitled to a heavenly reward (1 Cor 9:17).

Questions 4-5. Paul does not condemn earning money but rather *loving* money. Because Jesus had taught that we cannot love both God and money (see Mt 6:24), Paul knew that money can become a false god that lures us away from Jesus Christ and receives the kind of devotion that should be reserved for God alone. Those who love money and riches may receive many temporal rewards, but because they are guilty of idolatry their spiritual lives become a shambles.

Question 8. Many Christians think God wants us to lead unhappy, austere lives of toil and servitude. Paul shatters that notion in verse 17 by describing God as the one who "richly provides us with everything for our enjoyment." Everything good in life is a gift from our heavenly Father, who loves us and wants us to enjoy the best he has to offer (see Jas 1:17).

Question 9. Paul's investment strategy is simple: He urges us to generously invest our time, money and other resources in the lives of others so that we can receive heavenly dividends. He realizes that those who work only for temporal wealth invest in something that is uncertain and fleeting. But those who work for heavenly rewards invest in that which is certain and eternal.

Question 10. Be sure to leave enough time for this question. Encourage group members to think of specific areas in which they could become "rich in good deeds," more "generous" with their time, money and other resources and more "willing to share" with others what God has given to them (v. 18).

Study 4. Living in Hope. 1 Peter 1:3-12.

Purpose: To be filled with a childlike sense of joy and anticipation as we think about seeing Jesus Christ and living in our eternal home.

Question 2. This question isn't as simple as it sounds. People will probably respond initially by saying that we have a living hope because Jesus Christ is alive and embodies our hopes—which, of course, is true. But the Scriptures encourage us to think more deeply. The New Testament emphasizes that because we are united with Christ, or "in Christ," then we share in all the good that has happened to him since his resurrection from the dead. Because he was raised from the dead, we know that we too will one day be raised to live eternally. Because he has been exalted to the place of highest honor, we too will one day be glorified. And because he has entered heaven on our behalf, we too will join him there to live forever in the presence of God. All of our hopes are bound up in Christ, our living Savior.

Question 3. Have fun with this question. Think of the incredible joy and amazement people feel when they win the lottery or the Publishers Clearing House Sweepstakes. By using a word like *inheritance*, Peter is trying to tap into those feelings of joy in order to give us a sense of wonder and excitement about what God plans to give us.

Questions 4-5. Peter uses the word *trials* rather than *persecutions* or *tribulations* because he is thinking of the wide variety of ways Christians suffer because of their faith in Jesus Christ. Encourage your group to think broadly too.

The following quote helps to clarify Peter's image of gold being refined by fire: "When gold is refined, its impurities are removed by a fiery process. Though extremely durable, it belongs to the perishing world-order. Faith, which is more valuable than gold because it lasts longer and reaches beyond this temporal order, is purified in the tests of life. Gold, not faith, is presently highly valued by people. But God will set his stamp of approval on faith that has been tested and will show this when Christ is revealed. Then believers will openly share in the praise, glory, and honor of God" (*Zondervan NIV Bible Commentary*, vol. 2, *New Testament*, ed. Kenneth L. Barker and John Kohlenberger III [Grand Rapids: Zondervan, 1994], pp. 1043-44).

Question 8. The word *serving* emphasizes that the Old Testament is of value to the church, not just to the people to whom it was originally written. It is especially important as a record of the history of redemption—God's plan of salvation that found its ultimate fulfillment in Jesus Christ.

Question 9. Edwin A. Blum writes, "The Scriptures reveal that the angels have intense interest in human salvation. They observed Jesus in his early life (1 Tim 3:16); they rejoice at the conversion of a sinner (Lk 15:10); they will rejoice in songs of praise at the completion of redemption (Rev 5:11-14). The expression to 'long to look' means 'to stoop over to look' (cf. Lk 24:12; Jn 20:5, 11; Jas 1:25). It implies a willingness to exert or inconvenience oneself to obtain a better perspective. The specific tense used means continuous regard rather than a quick look. The Bible says nothing about salvation for angels. On the contrary, they learn about it from the church (Eph 3:10); and they serve the church (Heb 1:14)" (*NIV Bible Commentary,* p. 1044).

Study 5. Longing for Glory. Romans 8:18-27.

Purpose: To grasp what heavenly glory is, so that we can become more excited and expectant about it.

Group discussion. C. S. Lewis explains his concept of glory when he writes: "The promise of glory is the promise, almost incredible and only possible by the work of Christ, that some of us, that any of us who really chooses, shall actually survive that examination, shall find approval, shall please God. To please God . . . to be a real ingredient in the divine happiness . . . to be loved by God, not merely pitied, but delighted in as an artist delights in his work or a father in a son—it seems impossible, a weight or burden of glory which our thoughts can hardly sustain. But so it is" (*The Weight of Glory,* p. 13).

Question 1. Group members should mention the words "sufferings" (v. 18), "frustration" (v. 20), "bondage to decay" (v. 21), "groaning" (v. 22), "pains of childbirth" (v. 22), "groan inwardly" (v. 23) and "weakness" (v. 26). Paul is very realistic about the struggles of living in a fallen world.

Question 3. Think about the various ways in which our planet, and those who inhabit it, suffers from generation to generation: through death, disease, famine, pollution, poverty, natural disasters, personal frustration, lack of fulfillment and so on.

Question 4. Paul's concept of salvation is comprehensive, because he looks forward to a day in which the entire universe will be redeemed. This redemption includes not only the resurrection of those who believe in Christ but also the restoration of the physical universe. We will not spend eternity floating in the clouds but rather on a totally renovated earth (see 2 Pet 3:10-13; Rev 21:1-8).

Question 5. In his book *Inside Out,* Dr. Larry Crabb writes:

> Modern Christianity, in dramatic reversal of its biblical form, promises to relieve the pain of living in a fallen world. The mes-sage, whether it's from fundamentalists requiring us to live by a favored set of rules or from charismatics urging a deeper surren-

der to the Spirit's power, is too often the same: The promise of bliss is for NOW! Complete satisfaction can be ours this side of Heaven. . . . The effect of such teaching is to blunt the painful reality of what it's like to live as part of an imperfect, and sometimes evil, community. We learn to pretend that we feel now what we cannot feel until Heaven. ([Colorado Springs: Nav-Press, 1988], pp. 13-14.)

Question 6. Of all the expressions Paul uses to describe our future hope, the phrase "adoption as sons" is probably the one that is most difficult to comprehend. The *New Bible Dictionary* explains that "adoption in the NT has as its background not Roman law, in which its chief aim was to continue the adoptive parents line, but Jewish custom, which conferred the benefits of the family on the adoptee. . . . The adopted son of God possesses all family rights, including access to the Father (Rom 8:15) and sharing with Christ in the divine inheritance (Rom 8:17). The presence of the Spirit of God is both the instrument (Rom 8:14) and the consequence (Gal 4:6) of this sonship" (*New Bible Dictionary: Second Edition*, ed. J. D. Douglas [Downers Grove, Ill.: InterVarsity Press, 1982], p. 17).

Question 8. Paul's statements in verses 26-27 are incredible and astounding. As we groan inwardly because of our weaknesses and sufferings, the Holy Spirit identifies with us so strongly that he too groans with us and prays for us far more effectively than we could pray for ourselves. And because his prayers perfectly represent the will of the Father, we can be assured that the Spirit's prayers will be answered.

Study 6. The Ultimate Victory. 1 Corinthians 15:35-58.

Purpose: To explore the great and encouraging hope of the resurrection.

Question 1. Paul uses three analogies from the physical world. The first analogy is that of a seed, which "dies" and then gives birth to a new and different kind of "body." The second analogy is that of "flesh," which is different for men, animals, birds and fish, thereby showing that God is capable of making a new and different kind of flesh for our resurrection bodies. The third analogy is that of earthly "bodies," such as mountains or oceans, and heavenly "bodies," such as the moon and stars. For Paul this proves that God is capable of taking matter and arranging it in a great variety of forms—including the form of our resurrection bodies. In their skepticism the Corinthians overlook God's incredible creativity and power.

Question 2. Verses 42-44 are filled with contrasts: perishable/imperishable, dishonor/glory, weakness/power, natural/spiritual. Encourage your group to explore the implications of these contrasts. "The terms 'natural' and 'spiritual' in verse 44 use the identical language Paul has already used in 2:6-16 to indicate the difference between Christians and non-Christians. In this context, the contrast might better be indicated by translating the adjectives as 'natural' and 'supernatural'" (Craig Blomberg, *1 Corinthians,* NIV Application Commentary [Grand Rapids: Zondervan, 1994], p. 316).

Question 3. This is a question to have fun with but, if you think that it would make your group uncomfortable, feel free to skip it.

Question 4. Paul views the whole of humanity in one of two categories. The first category includes Adam and all of his descendants, whose bodies were formed from the dust of the earth. The second category includes Jesus Christ and all who believe in him. Just as Christ came from heaven and now possesses a resurrection body fit for heaven, so too all who are "in Christ" will receive bodies like his.

Question 6. Paul tells us that our current bodies are not fit for the kingdom of God. They are made of *perishable* materials—flesh and blood—when they need to be made out of *imperishable*, supernatural materials. Likewise, our current bodies are *mortal*—easily killed or destroyed—when they need to become *immortal*—incapable of death or destruction.

I love the way that C. S. Lewis describes heaven in his book *The Great Divorce*. When a bus-load of people take a trip to heaven, the first thing they discover is that everything there is made of very solid stuff. A man bends down to pluck a daisy and discovers that he cannot break its stem. He tugs and pulls until he is sweating and then realizes that he has lost much of the skin on his hand. Then he tries to pick up a young, tender leaf lying in the grass and finds it is so heavy that he can just barely budge it—but he has to drop it immediately because of its enormous weight. As the people from the bus walk on the grass, they discover that the blades don't even bend under their feet, and the dew drops aren't even disturbed. Then—to their shock and horror—they realize that in contrast to the heavenly landscape they all look like ghosts or phantoms. Paul tells us that our current bodies aren't capable of living in such a place. But Christ has promised us new, glorious bodies that are just as *durable* and *solid* and *eternal* as the kingdom we will inherit!

Questions 8-9. Jesus Christ has removed both the sting and victory of death. He has taken away the victory of death through his own resurrection and the promise of resurrection for all who believe in him. He has taken away the sting of death because all who die in Christ do not really die in the ultimate sense but rather go immediately to be with Christ in heaven (see Jn 11:25-26). Dwight L. Moody once said, "One day you will read that D. L. Moody is dead. *Don't you believe it!* At that moment I will be more alive than I ever have been here on earth." Any friend or relative of yours who has died in Christ is more alive now than they ever were when you knew them. That's not a pious fiction or an opiate for the masses. It is a *fact* that should give us great encouragement and hope.

Study 7. The Return of the King. 1 Thessalonians 4:13—5:11.
Purpose: To view the second coming as a living hope that restructures our thinking and reorders our lives.

Question 1. Death may seem normal in our fallen world, but in fact death came into the world because of sin (Gen 2:17) and will be eventually abolished by Jesus Christ (1 Cor 15:54). Even now Jesus has radically transformed the nature of death for those who believe in him. Because of the resurrection, believers can view death the way they view sleep: an experience that is merely temporary. Jesus himself encouraged us to view death this way when he raised Jairus's daughter from the dead (Mk 5:21-43). When Jesus saw the mourners crying loudly and wailing, he said to them: "Why all this commotion and wailing? The child is not dead but asleep" (v. 39).

Question 2. Paul's statements in verse 13 show us that we should avoid two extremes. The first extreme is to have such a superspiritual view of death that we suppress our grief—or deny others their legitimate need to grieve—and make pious statements such as, "Isn't it wonderful that [the person's name] is with the Lord!" Although it may indeed be wonderful for the person who has died, it is *not* so wonderful for those who have lost someone they loved deeply. The second extreme is to grieve like those who have no hope (1 Thess 4:13). Our grief must always be tempered by the hope and encouragement we have through Jesus Christ, who has promised to raise believers from the dead (v. 14).

Question 3. Paul assures the Thessalonians that those who have died in Christ before his coming will not be forgotten. On the contrary, they will be the first to be resurrected. The sequence will be as follows: (1) The Lord will come down from heaven; (2) he will give a loud command, presumably commanding those who have died to rise from the dead; (3) his command will be accompanied by the voice of the archangel (this may be Michael, see Jude 9) and the trumpet of God; (4) those who have died in Christ will be the first to rise and meet the Lord; (5) those who are still alive at the Lord's Coming will be "caught up together with them in the clouds to meet the Lord in the air."

There are some who believe that the event Paul is describing here is not the second coming of Christ but rather a secret "rapture" (from the Latin Vulgate rendering of "caught up" in v. 17) of the church that will occur a few years before the Lord's return. Although this passage can certainly be made to fit into such a view, there is nothing in the passage itself that would distinguish this event from the second coming of Christ, and this seems to be the most natural way of interpreting Paul's reference to "the coming of the Lord" (v. 15). Yet Paul's primary purpose for writing this passage isn't to settle finer points of doctrine but rather to encourage us. Help the group to focus on the encouraging nature of this passage, therefore, and try to avoid getting entangled in controversy.

Question 4. Jesus himself not only taught that he would come like a thief in the night (Mt 24:43) but also warned that "no one knows about that day or hour, not even the angels in heaven, nor the Son, but only the Father" (Mt 24:36). He repeated this fact two more times in the same passage: "You do not know on what day your Lord will come" (v. 42) and "The Son of Man will come at an hour when you do not expect him" (v. 44). Yet in spite of these statements there have been those in almost every generation who have presumed to know the timing of the Lord's return.

Question 7. We need to realize that the biblical passages that speak of the Lord's return emphasize judgment as well as salvation. That fact should motivate us to tell others about the salvation that is freely available through Jesus Christ—just as we would surely warn them of a coming tornado, hurricane, flood or other natural disaster so that they could be prepared.

Study 8. When All Things Become New. Revelation 21:1-8.

Purpose: To consider the better world Christ promises those who believe in him and why it offers us such incredible hope.

Question 2. Normally, we think of heaven as the place we go to after we die—and obviously it's not here on earth. But the Bible teaches that we will *not* spend eternity floating around in the clouds, chasing moonbeams and playing harps. Heaven as we normally think of it is only a *temporary* home. Scripture teaches that we will spend eternity on a recreated and renovated earth in our resurrection bodies.

After Jesus returns, he will transform not only our lowly bodies but also this fallen earth, making it even more beautiful than the first earth he created. Imagine that—the new earth will be more majestic than the Grand Canyon, more lush than the Brazilian rain forest, more breathtaking than Yosemite National Park, more exotic than Hawaii.

In C. S. Lewis's book *The Last Battle* one of the characters describes the new earth this way: "I have come home at last! This is my real country! I belong here. This is the land I have been looking for all my life, though I never knew it till now. The reason why we loved the old Narnia is that it sometimes looked a little like this" (C. S. Lewis, *The Last Battle* [New York: Collier Books, 1956], p. 171).

Questions 3-4. Christianity is fundamentally relational. We were created and designed to live in an intimate relationship with God and others. Because marriage is potentially the most intimate relationship on earth, the biblical writers frequently compare our ultimate relationship with God to a marriage.

People have enormous expectations for marriage—at least initially. If you listen to most love songs, you'll find that they have almost a religious quality about them: "You are my destiny." "I'll love you for all eternity." "You're my reason for living." "You give me hope to carry on." Unfortunately, even the best marriage relationship can't meet these lofty expectations, and the worst leaves them shattered in ruins. Yet in heaven our expectations *will* be met. The Bible says that the one we've always dreamed of is actually God himself. Notice what John writes in verse 3: "And I heard a loud voice from the throne saying, 'Now the dwelling of God is with men [and women], and he will live with them. They will be his people, and God himself will be with them and be their God.'" In other words, heaven is not primarily a *place* but a *Person*—the one person who can fulfill our deepest desires for intimacy.

Notice, however, that John also describes heaven as a city, not a quiet table for two. Although our greatest intimacy will be with the one we're married to—God himself—we will also have wonderful, fulfilling relationships with each other.

Question 5. John writes, "He will wipe every tear from their eyes. There will be no more death or mourning or crying or pain, for the old order of things has passed away."

A number of years ago a movie came out called *Tender Mercies*. The main character, played by Robert Duvall, was an alcoholic, a has-been country-western songwriter who's down on his luck, divorced and hasn't seen his teenaged daughter since she was a baby. Then one day he happens upon a small motel and gas station owned by a widow and her young son. They take the man in, and his life begins to turn around. He stops drinking for the first time in years. The boy becomes like a son to him. He falls in love with the woman, and they decide to get married. He even becomes a Christian and is baptized in the country church the family attends. His joy is complete when he gets to see his daughter, and the two of them promise to renew their relationship.

But then, just as everything seems to be going so well, he receives word that his daughter has been killed in an automobile accident. His wife finds him later, out in the garden, and they begin to talk. Although I cannot recall his exact words, he said in essence: "I just don't understand anything. Why did God bring me here? Why did you take me in and love me and welcome me into your family? And just when things were going so well, why did God take my daughter? I just don't trust happiness. I never have, and I never will."

In this life, it's almost impossible to experience joy without sorrow, laughter without tears, pleasure without pain. *But one day we will.* "He who is seated on the throne says, 'I am making everything new! Write this down, for these words are trustworthy and true.'"

Question 6. Allow group members to answer this according to their own comfort level—in generalities in relation to life on earth or very specifically to their own life.

Question 7. For me it is helpful to realize that even the most irreligious, immoral person may be driven by religious impulses. Whenever people try to fill the void in their lives through materialism, personal achievement and recognition, sensuality or substance abuse, they are, in fact, revealing their inner cravings for God! Jesus recognized this kind of craving in the woman at the well (Jn 4) and in many other people who, on the surface, did not appear to be likely candidates for conversion.

Now or Later. There is a wonderful passage in *The Last Battle* that for me captures the essence of heaven and all that you have been reading in this passage: "And for us this is the end of all the stories, and we can most truly say that they all lived happily ever after. But for them it was only the beginning of the real story. All their life in this world and all their adventures in Narnia had only been the cover and title page: now at last they were beginning Chapter One of the Great Story which no one on earth has read: which goes on forever: in which every chapter is better than the one before" (p. 184).

———————————

Jack Kuhatschek was formerly an executive vice president and publisher for Baker Publishing Group in Grand Rapids, Michigan. He is the author of many Bible study guides, including twelve in the LifeBuilder series, and the books Applying the Bible *and* The Superman Syndrome.